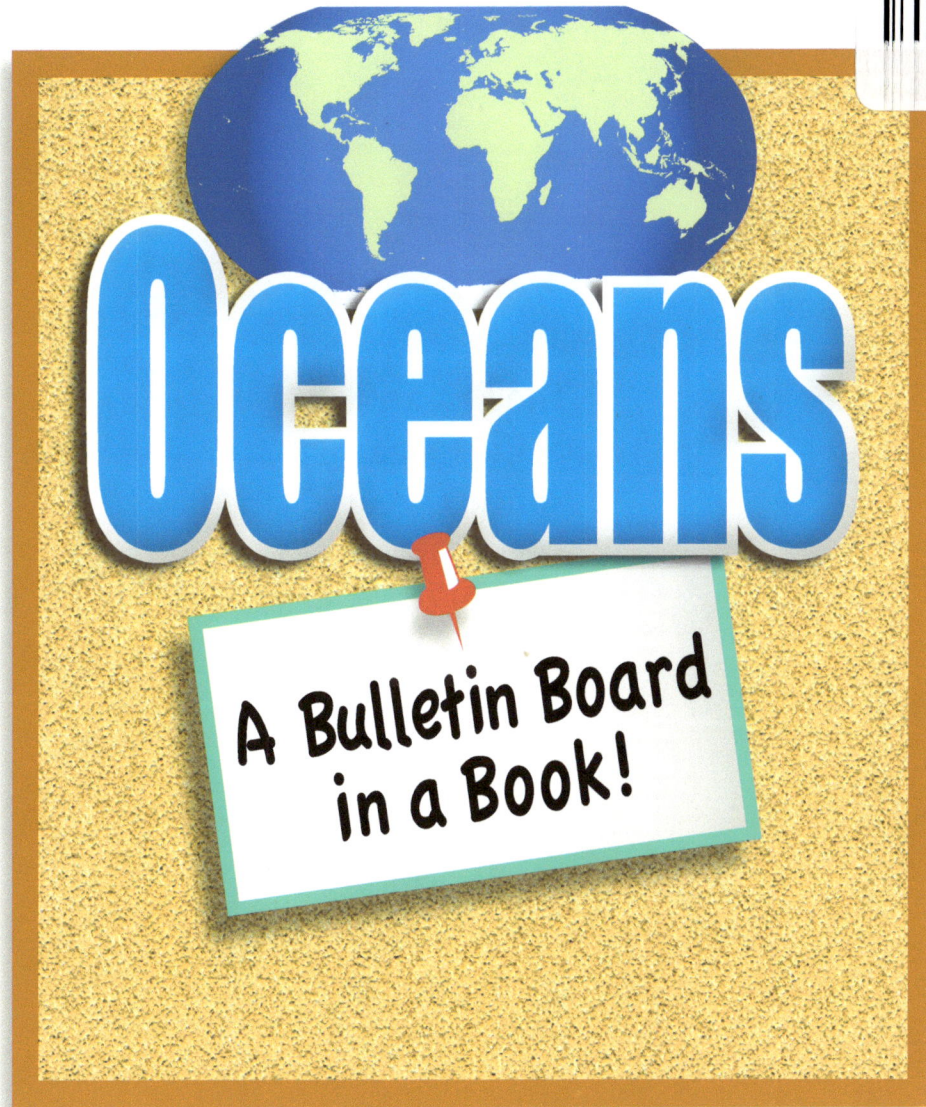

Oceans

A Bulletin Board in a Book!

Sunflower education

Exceptional Books for Teachers and Parents

Editorial
Sunflower Education

Design
Cynthia Hannon Design

Illustrations:
Cover and interior images: © Shutterstock Images LLC

ISBN-13: 978-1-937166-15-1
ISBN-10: 1-937166-15-5

Table of Contents

To the Teacher

Activity Sheets
The Oceans
Pacific Ocean
Atlantic Ocean
Indian Ocean
Southern Ocean
Arctic Ocean

Posters
Oceans
Ocean Facts
Pacific Ocean
Pacific Ocean Map
Atlantic Ocean
Atlantic Ocean Map
Indian Ocean
Indian Ocean Map
Southern Ocean
Southern Ocean Map
Arctic Ocean
Arctic Ocean Map
Remember the Oceans!

To the Teacher

Oceans: A Bulletin Board in a Book! consists of two main parts:
bulletin-board posters and student activity sheets. They are designed to be used together.

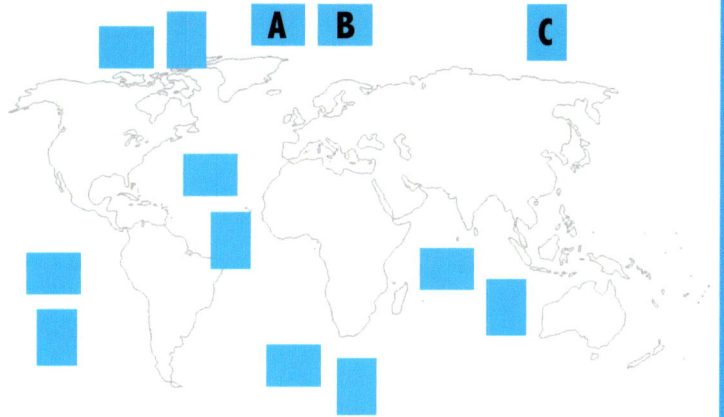

There are 13 posters:
- 1—Oceans (title poster **A**)
- 1—Oceans Facts (subtitle poster **B**)
- 5—Ocean Facts Posters
- 5—Ocean Map Posters
- 1—Remember the Oceans! Poster (**C**)

There are 6 student activity sheets:
- 1—on oceans in general
- 5—ocean-specific

Place posters to show relative locations of oceans.

❶ Post the Bulletin-Board Display
- Copy the posters or cut them out.
- See the illustration for suggested layout.
- Post the Oceans (title poster) and Oceans Facts (subtitle poster) posters together to form the top or central part of the display.
- Pair each Ocean Facts Poster with its corresponding Ocean Map Poster.
- Post the Remember the Oceans! Poster in a prominent place.

❷ Discuss Oceans with Students
- Lead a discussion about the oceans. Allow students time to peruse the posters. Ensure students understand the concepts of area, longest distances, and depth.
- Encourage students to memorize the names and sizes of the oceans. Work with students to complete the Remember the Oceans! Poster. Explain that the letters are the first letter of each ocean's name and that the letters represent the oceans from largest to smallest. Encourage students to come up with a memorable phrase (for example, "Pete And Irene Sing Along") as a mnemonic device.
- Focus students' attention on the small locator maps on the Ocean Facts Posters (point out the red indicator arrows) and the larger Ocean Map Posters. Encourage them to memorize the shapes and locations of the oceans.

❸ Share the Activity sheets
- All of the activity sheets can be completed using information from the posters. Consider having students complete the activity sheets either as assessment or with access to the bulletin board.
- Students can complete the activity sheets individually or with partners.

Emphasize the vast sizes of the oceans, the great distances across them, and their fantastic depth. Have fun sharing the world with your students!

Worksheet Answers

The Oceans
1. 1. Arctic; 2. Pacific; 3. Atlantic; 4. Southern; 5. Indian.
2. 5, 2, 3, 1, 4
3. Reward thoughtful responses.
4. Verify correct answers.
5. Reward earnest answers.

Pacific Ocean
1. X should be on the Pacific Ocean.
2. 15,000 miles
3. 13,000 feet
4. calm and gentle
5. North America, South America, Antarctica, Africa, Asia.

Atlantic Ocean
1. X should be on the Atlantic Ocean.
2. 13,000 miles
3. 12,000 feet
4. The ancient Romans
5. North America, South America, Europe, Africa.

Indian Ocean
1. X should be on the Indian Ocean.
2. 6,200 miles
3. 13,000 feet
4. India
5. Africa, Asia, Australia.

Southern Ocean
1. X should be on the Southern Ocean.
2. Antarctica
3. 15,000 feet
4. 23,737 feet
5. Antarctica

Arctic Ocean
1. X should be on the Arctic Ocean.
2. 2,600 miles
3. 4,000 feet
4. It is frozen into ice
5. North America, Europe, Asia.

The Oceans

1 Write the name of each ocean by the correct number below.

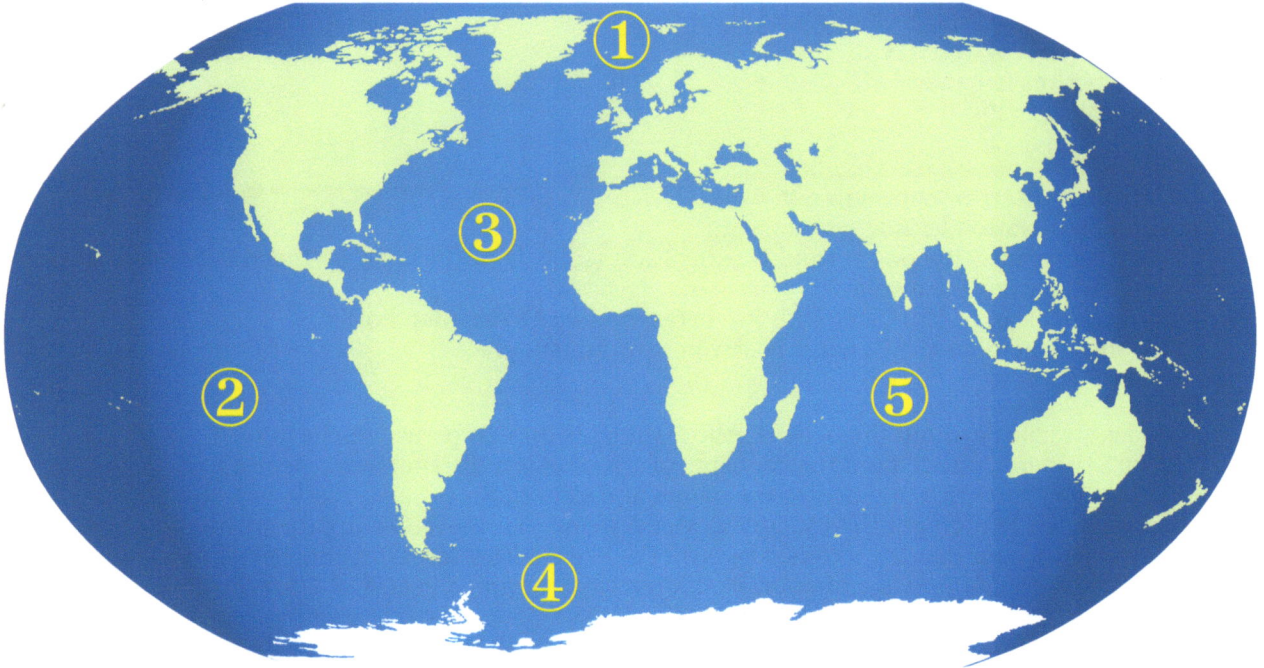

① _____

② _____

③ _____

④ _____

⑤ _____

2 Number the oceans from 1 to 5. Write 1 next to the biggest ocean.
Write 2 next to the second-biggest ocean.
Keep going until you number all 5.

____ **Arctic Ocean**   ____ **Pacific Ocean**

____ **Atlantic Ocean**   ____ **Southern Ocean**

____ **Indian Ocean**

3 Write something you think is interesting about the oceans.

_____

_____

_____

4 Which ocean do you live closest to?

_____

5 Tell why you would like to see the sea. Or tell about a time you saw the sea.

_____

_____

_____

Pacific Ocean

1 Where is the Pacific Ocean? Put an X on the map to show where the Pacific Ocean is.

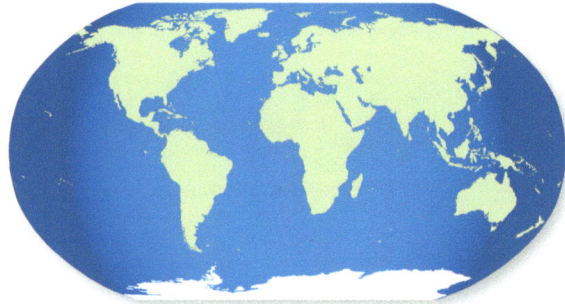

2 What is the longest distance across the Pacific Ocean?

_____

3 What is the average depth of the Pacific Ocean?

_____

4 What does the word "pacific" mean?

_____

5 Which continents border the Pacific Ocean?

_____

_____

_____

Atlantic Ocean

1 Where is the Atlantic Ocean? Put an X on the map to show where the Atlantic Ocean is.

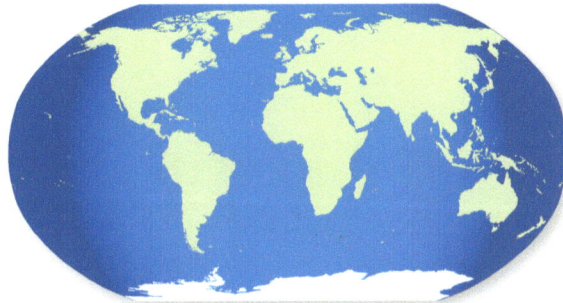

2 What is the longest distance across the Atlantic Ocean?

_____

3 What is the average depth of the Atlantic Ocean?

_____

4 Who gave the Atlantic Ocean its name?

_____

5 Which continents border the Atlantic Ocean?

_____

_____

_____

Indian Ocean

1 Where is the Indian Ocean? Put an X on the map to show where the Indian Ocean is.

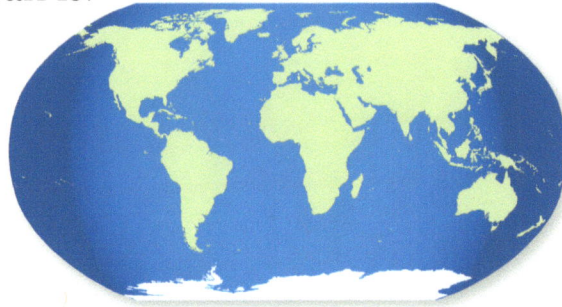

2 What is the longest distance across the Indian Ocean?

_____

3 What is the average depth of the Indian Ocean?

_____

4 What is the Indian Ocean named after?

_____

5 Which continents border the Indian Ocean?

_____

_____

_____

Southern Ocean

1 Where is the Southern Ocean? Put an X on the map to show where the Southern Ocean is.

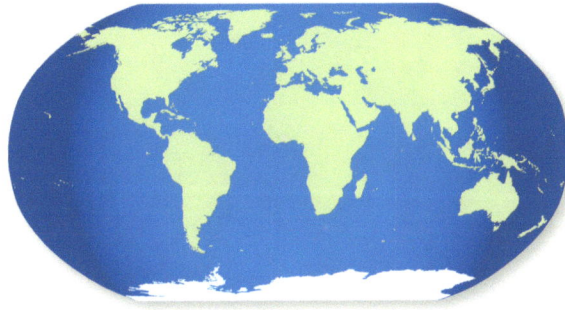

2 What does the Southern Ocean surround?

_____

3 What is the average depth of the Southern Ocean?

_____

4 How deep is the deepest spot of the Southern Ocean?

_____

5 Which continent borders the Southern Ocean?

_____

_____

_____

Arctic Ocean

1 Where is the Arctic Ocean? Put an X on the map to show where the Arctic Ocean is.

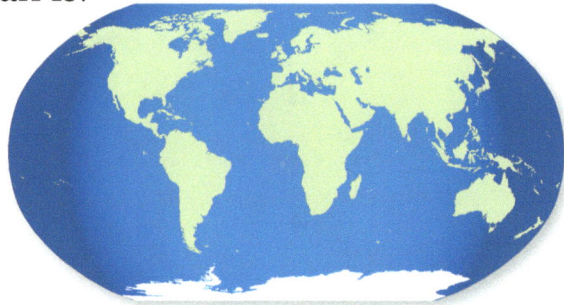

2 What is the longest distance across the Arctic Ocean?

_____

3 What is the average depth of the Arctic Ocean?

_____

4 Why can you walk on parts of the Arctic Ocean?

_____

_____

5 Which continents border the Arctic Ocean?

_____

_____

_____

Oceans

Most of the Earth is covered by water. This great body of water is called *the world ocean*. The world ocean is also called *the sea*.

The continents divide the world ocean into five parts. Each part is an ocean with its own name.

Pacific Ocean • Atlantic Ocean • Indian Ocean • Southern Ocean • Arctic Ocean

Oceans Facts

How Big? Oceans cover more than two-thirds of the Earth.

How Deep? The oceans have an average depth of 13,000 feet. The deepest point in the ocean is 35,840 feet deep.

How Important? Oceans are needed for life on Earth. This is because the oceans help keep the air at a good temperature. They also provide moisture for rain.

Did You Know? People need the oceans. The oceans provide us with food. Ships carry people and goods between continents. People like to ride boats and swim in the oceans. Half of all the people in the world live close to an ocean.

The Pacific Ocean

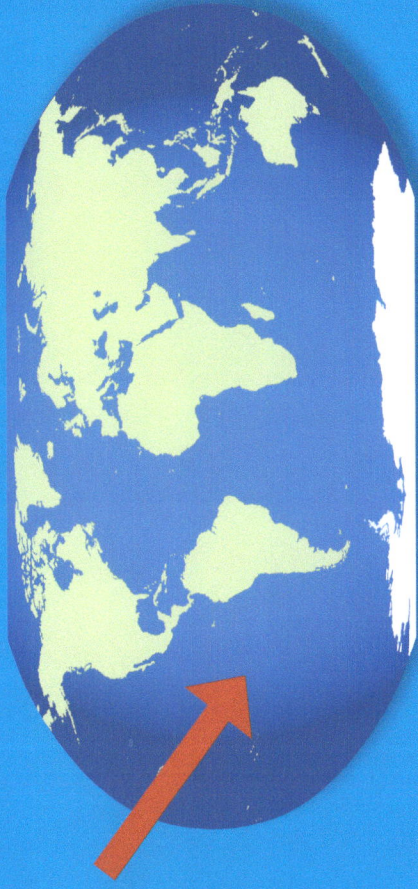

How Big?

The Pacific Ocean has an area of 66 million square miles. The Pacific is the largest ocean.

How Far?

The Pacific Ocean's longest distances are 8,600 miles north to south and 15,000 miles east to west.

How Deep?

The Pacific Ocean has an average depth of 13,000 feet. Its deepest spot is 35,840 feet deep.

Did You Know?

Ferdinand Magellan was an explorer. He sailed the Pacific. He found calm water and gentle winds. "Pacific" means calm and gentle.

The Pacific Ocean

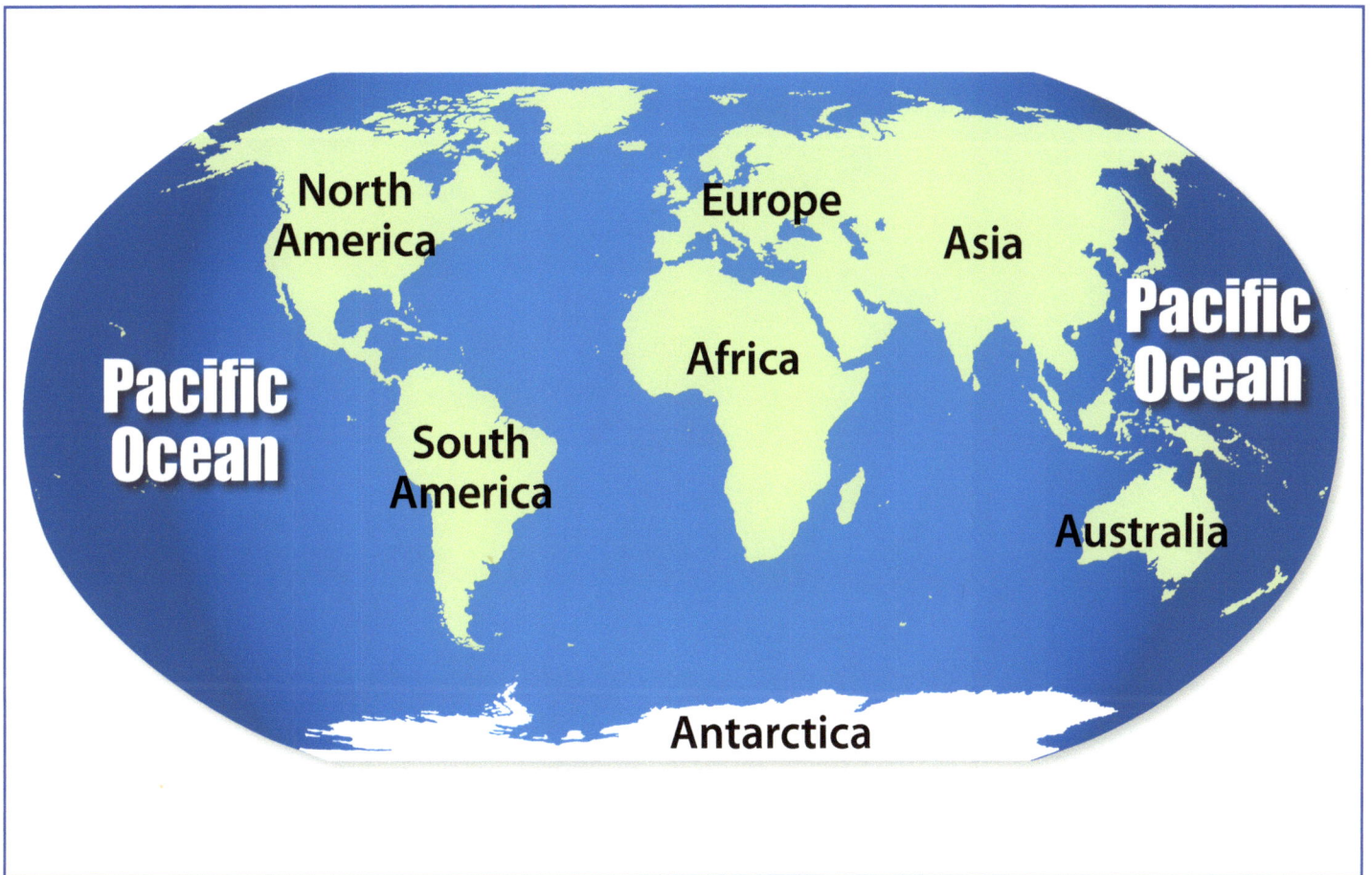

North America

Europe

Asia

Pacific Ocean

Africa

Pacific Ocean

South America

Australia

Antarctica

The Atlantic Ocean

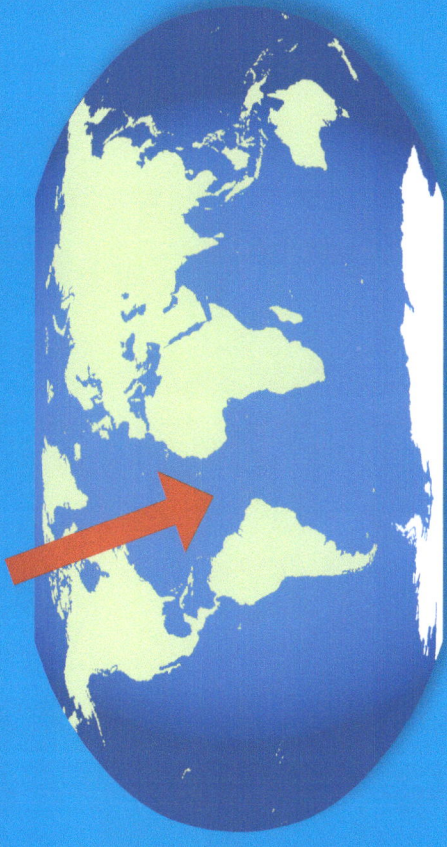

How Big?

The Atlantic Ocean has an area of 34 million square miles. The Atlantic is the second-largest ocean.

How Far?

The Atlantic Ocean's longest distances are 13,000 miles north to south and 5,500 miles east to west.

How Deep?

The Atlantic Ocean has an average depth of 12,000 feet. Its deepest spot is 28,232 feet deep.

Did You Know?

The ancient Romans named the Atlantic. The Atlas Mountains were at the edge of their land. Atlantic means "beyond the Atlas Mountains."

The Atlantic Ocean

North America

Europe

Atlantic Ocean

Africa

South America

The Indian Ocean

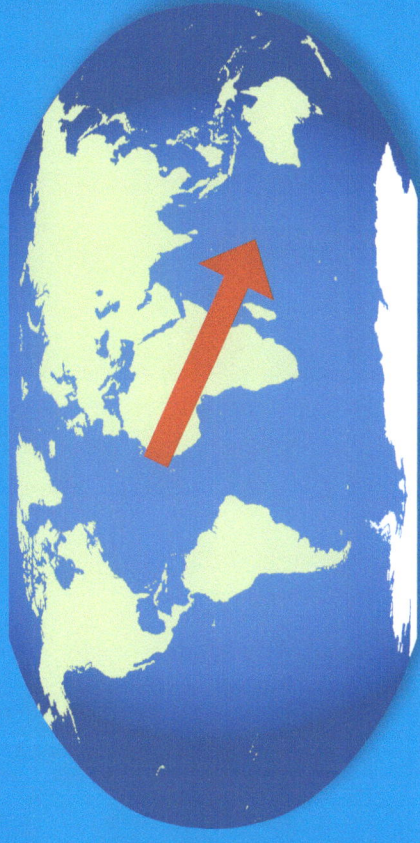

How Big?

The Indian Ocean has an area of 27 million square miles. The Indian is the third-largest ocean.

How Far?

The Indian Ocean's longest distances are 5,500 miles north to south and 6,200 miles east to west.

How Deep?

The Indian Ocean has an average depth of 13,000 feet. Its deepest spot is 23,812 feet deep.

Did You Know?

The Indian Ocean is named after India. India is a huge piece of land that sticks into the ocean from the continent of Asia.

The Indian Ocean

Asia

Africa

Indian Ocean

Australia

The Southern Ocean

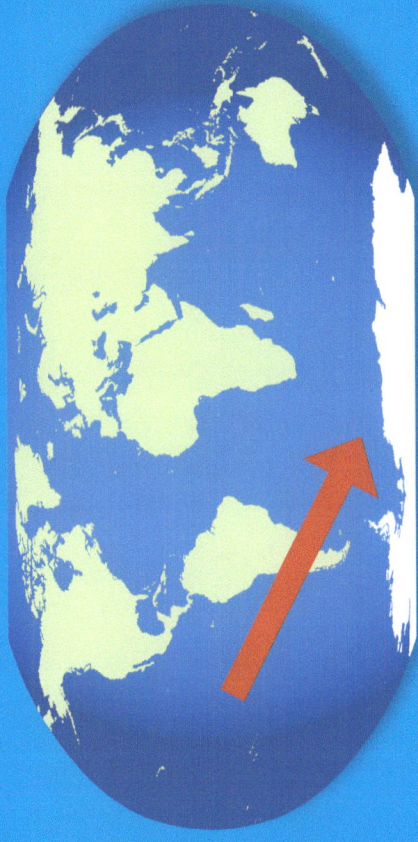

How Big?

The Southern Ocean has an area of 9 million square miles. The Southern Ocean is the fourth-largest ocean.

How Deep?

The Southern Ocean has an average depth of 15,000 feet. Its deepest spot is 23,737 feet deep.

Did You Know?

You can not sail "across" the Southern Ocean. This is because the continent of Antarctica is in the middle of the Southern Ocean. The Southern Ocean surrounds Antarctica.

The Southern Ocean

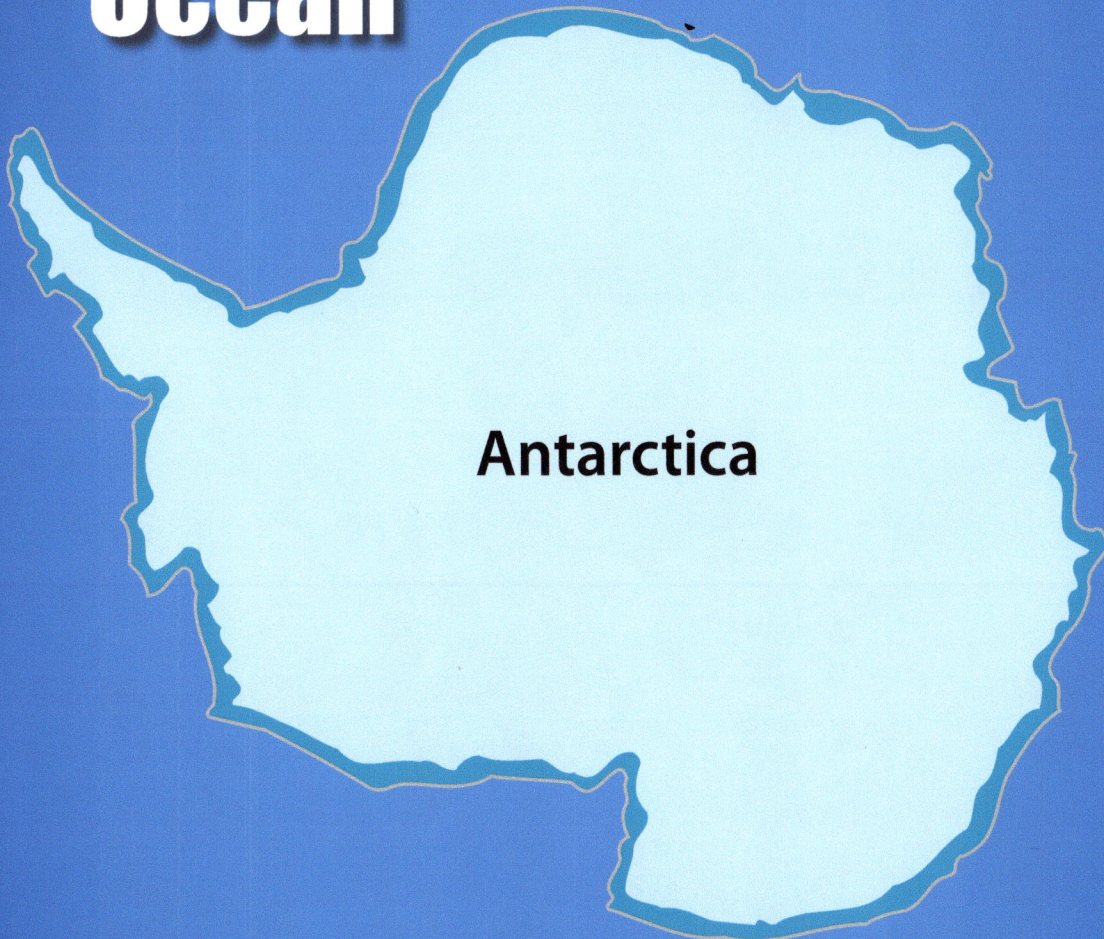

Southern
Ocean

Antarctica

The Arctic Ocean

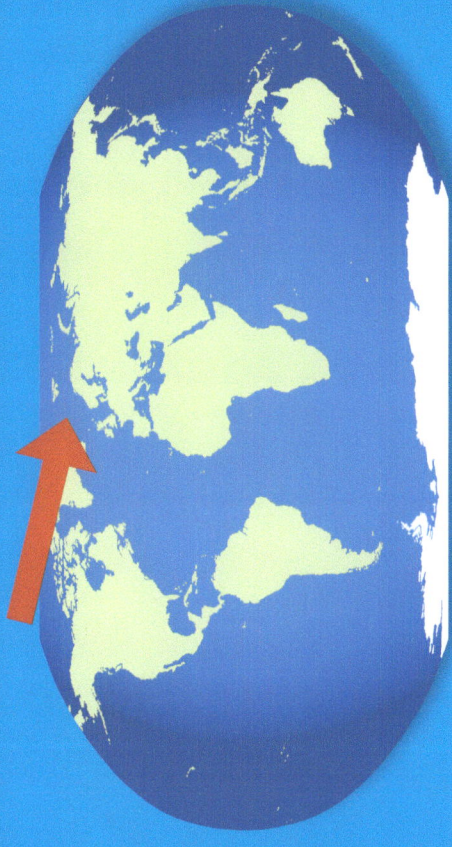

How Big?

The Arctic Ocean has an area of 5 million square miles. The Arctic is the smallest ocean.

How Far?

The Arctic Ocean's longest distance is 2,600 miles across.

How Deep?

The Arctic Ocean has an average depth of 4,000 feet. Its deepest spot is 15,305 feet deep.

Did You Know?

The Arctic Ocean is in a part of the world that is always cold. Much of the surface of the ocean is frozen into ice. You can walk on the ocean!

The Arctic Ocean

Remember the Oceans!

P _____

A _____

I _____

S _____

A _____

www.ingramcontent.com/pod-product-compliance
Lightning Source LLC
Chambersburg PA
CBHW060836270326
41933CB00002B/102